Allan Ahlberg

THE BUCKET

Memories of an Inattentive Childhood

WITH ILLUSTRATIONS BY

Janet Ahlberg

Fritz Wegner

Charlotte Voake

Jessica Ahlberg

PENGUIN BOOKS

PENGUIN BOOKS

Published by the Penguin Group
Penguin Books Ltd, 80 Strand, London WC2R ORL, England
Penguin Group (USA) Inc., 375 Hudson Street, New York, New York 10014, USA
Penguin Group (Canada), 90 Eglinton Avenue East, Suite 700, Toronto, Ontario, Canada M4P 2Y3
(a division of Pearson Penguin Canada Inc.)
Penguin Ireland, 25 St Stephen's Green, Dublin 2, Ireland (a division of Penguin Books Ltd)
Penguin Group (Australia), 707 Collins Street, Melbourne, Victoria 3008, Australia
(a division of Pearson Australia Group Pty Ltd)
Penguin Books India Pvt Ltd, 11 Community Centre, Panchsheel Park, New Delhi - 110 017, India
Penguin Group (NZ), 67 Apollo Drive, Rosedale, Auckland 0632, New Zealand
(a division of Pearson New Zealand Ltd)
Penguin Books (South Africa) (Pty) Ltd, Block D, Rosebank Office Park,
181 Jan Smuts Avenue, Parktown North, Gauteng 2193, South Africa

Penguin Books Ltd, Registered Offices: 80 Strand, London WC2R ORL, England

www.penguin.com

First published by Viking 2013
Published in Penguin Books 2014
001

Text copyright © Allan Ahlberg, 2013
Original illustrations copyright © Jessica Ahlberg, 2013
All rights reserved

The acknowledgements on p. xi constitute an extension of this copyright page

The moral right of the author has been asserted

Printed in Great Britain by Clays Ltd, St Ives plc

ISBN: 978-0-241-96566-5

www.greenpenguin.co.uk

BOROUGH OF OLDBURY EDUCATION COMMITTEE.

ROOD END PRIMARY SCHOOL.

REPORT FOR HALF YEAR ENDING _December 1946._

Name _Ahlberg Allan_ Age _8 6/12 yrs._

Class _Form 2 A._ No. of Children in Class _55_

No. of Times Absent _1_ No. of Times Late _0_ _Excused._

Position in Class _20?_ Intelligence Test _-_

Subject.	Max. Mk.	Mk. Obt.	Position	Remarks.
Arithmetic	20	2	49	Very Poor
Mental Arithmetic	20	14	12	Very Fair
Composition	20	16	22	Good.
Spelling	20	15	21	Fairly Good.
Writing	20	14	41	" "
Reading	20	20	1	Excellent
Recitation	20	19	7	Very Good
Geography	20	18	6	" "
History	20	12	19	Very Fair
Elem. Science	20	15	13	Fairly Good
Art	20	14	30	Very Fair
Needle Work	-	-	-	
Craft	20	9	51	Fair
Scripture	20	19	4	Very Good
P.T.		4.		

GENERAL REMARKS. _Allan could do much better work. He is most-_
inattentive and dreamy at times

Class Teacher's Signature _B. Palmer._   Head Teacher's Signature _E. J. Reynolds_

Parent's Signature _G. H. Ahlberg._

BONSER & DAWES
SOLICITORS.

OLDBURY, 13 February 1939

Received of Mr & Mrs G. H. Ahlberg

the sum of Two pounds fifteen shillings and one penny

one cents in respect of the adoption by you of an infant

named George Allan, including fee for certificate

£ 2 . 15 . 1

If any part of the following mixture of truth and fiction strikes the reader as unconvincing, he has my permission to disregard it.

So Long, See You Tomorrow,
William Maxwell

Contents

Acknowledgements

JANET AHLBERG

Illustrations: pp. 21, 69, 103 from
   The Bear Nobody Wanted (1992)
   p. 27 from *Peepo!* (1981)
   pp. 31, 33, 95, 97 from *The Clothes Horse and
   Other Stories* (1987)

FRITZ WEGNER

Illustrations: p. 55 from
   Heard it in the Playground (1989)
   pp. 114, 116, 117, 121 from *Friendly Matches* (2001)

CHARLOTTE VOAKE

Illustrations: pp. 83, 84 from *The Mighty Slide* (1988)

JESSICA AHLBERG

Original illustrations published here for the first
   time: Cover, half title, title,
   pp. 45, 47, 48, 65, 79, 81, 86, 125 (age 6), 127,
   129, also endpaper

James Hogg – extract from 'A Boy's Song',
    p. 34
Sir John Millais – *Sir Isumbras at the Ford*,
    p. 36. The Lady Lever Art Gallery;
    reproduced courtesy National
    Museums Liverpool
G. E. Breary – *The Bear Nobody Wanted*
    (1944), pp. 100, 102, 105, 106

The author (*c.* 1942) with book.

Beginnings

I came from Battersea
In 1938
Delivered by a steam train
Forty minutes late.

Not the Dogs' Home, though.

My mother went to fetch me
By tram, then train
With Dad, as usual, working
Hopes's - Window Frames.

Or was it Danks's Boilers?

My mother had a shopping bag
Bootees, bottle, shawl
And knitting for the journey
Not much else at all.

A purse, I suppose, hat, glasses and such.

She struggled across London
Got lost near Waterloo
And came at last to the Orphanage
At twenty-five to two.

Early, even so, for a two o'clock appointment.

They sat her in the corridor
Left her there till three
Then gave her a couple of documents
A form to sign – and me.

She couldn't see to write. 'M'glasses needed wipers!'

Back then to Paddington
Weather wet and mild
Brand-new mother
Second-hand child.

Good condition, though; one previous owner.

And Mother clutched her secret
On her lap
From all the other passengers
All the way back.

Dad, still in his overalls, was on the platform.

He squeezed us in a cuddle
Gave me a clumsy kiss
He smelled of wood shavings and oil
Mum specially remembered this.

And me? Asleep, apparently. I'd had a busy day.*

In the early years of my childhood there was a war going on. The odd bomb meant for Coventry sometimes fell on us. My mother made me a den under the kitchen table, a solid table, a nest also of cushions and blankets. Soft toys. Toast. A cup of drink. It's what I most remember, not the bombs or the craters even, into one of which on my tricycle at speed I one time tumbled, but that little secret place with its green tablecloth hanging down, velvet tassels and a fringe. And the sounds of the kitchen: cups, plates, conversation. And the light through the fringe. The green light.

This is a book of short pieces in verse and prose, an attempt to recover or otherwise conjure up a particular time (the 1940s), a particular Black Country town (Oldbury) and a particular childhood (mine). There is, I will confess, some unreliability here. I start with good intentions and a true memory – day-old chicks, street lamps, a clip round the ear – but soon, often as not, the fictional habit kicks in and

3

*'Having a Baby', Collected Poems (2008).

I am led astray. One sentence lures me on to another, has the seeds of another in it, or is a template almost. Like knitting, that first row of stitches which sets up the rest. Or a rhyme reveals, or the need to avoid a rhyme reveals, some possibility. And I follow.

In 'The Richest Woman in the World' (page 72) which I have just completed there is a man in the Co-op serving my mother. I give him an apron, which I know he had, and place a pencil behind his ear, which I can only say I would like him to have had. He looks better with a pencil, in my opinion, more convincing, businesslike. He can tot up my mother's bill with it. There again, it's probably indelible. Yes, I think I detect a slight smudge now along his lower lip where he's been licking it. Like a young child, me, for instance (or you, for that matter), from those days, those remote, mysterious days. Eating liquorice.

The Bucket

I had a little bucket
Of brightly painted tin
Which I carried from the wash house
With my own river in.

I tipped the silver water
Where the soil was brown and hard
And made a little valley
In the communal yard.

I took some little soldiers
Some cows, a sheep or two
And placed them on the muddy bank
And told them what to do.

I kept my river flowing
(From the wash house to the sea)
Till my socks and shoes were soaking
And it was time for tea.

The river and the soldiers now
The bucket, all are gone
The wash house too is washed away
While time flows on.

But still I have a job to do
Some little tales to tell
And I'll bring my other bucket
To the Memory Well.

The Bacon Slicer

Sam Wooldridge was our butcher. I did not like his shop. He dealt, of course, in meat and menace. I could not see above the counter, but through various gaps the bloodied chopping blocks were visible. Cleavers and a multitude of knives. Hooks from the ceiling, half-carcasses and other cuts of pigs and cows suspended. Plucked, naked chickens tied up by their feet, a line of lifeless rabbits dangling with blood-red bulging eyes, yet wearing still their furry paws like slippers.

I did not like it (Bye, Baby Bunting, Daddy's gone a-hunting). A smell of blood and sawdust. Striped, blood-stained aprons on the butchers, one of whom (not Mr Wooldridge) had a blackened, shiny artificial fist where his left hand had been. He had chopped off his own hand! And yet he smiled and chatted with the customers, casually using his fist to hold a rack of chops or cutlets steady while he carved them up. And took the money with his other hand. And tinged the till.

I did not like it, pulled at my mother's coat for us to leave. Worst of all, in all that slaughterhouse - or operating theatre, I had lately had my tonsils out - there was The Bacon Slicer, a spinning, fiendish, circular blade that hummed to

7

itself, slicing the meat. It seemed like a person to me; animated. It was the noise, I suppose, that 'whoosh' of satisfaction with each slice. Also the smooth intelligence of it. It made no mistakes, no slicer ever sliced itself.

We'd leave at last, out in the street a better smell, of factories and canals, to breathe. And I would gaze back briefly – tugging again at my mother's coat, this time to detain her – at the only feature in Sam Wooldridge's that I ever liked, or cared to remember, or strove not to forget (those nightmarish rabbits). A model of a pig in the window in a butcher's apron and a butcher's hat. A cheerful pig with a smile on his face. Waving a cleaver.

Documentation

I have in my possession an improvised payslip, three inches by an inch and a half, brown paper, faded ink. 'Allan Ahlberg,' it says, 'Check N° 0000, Sunday April 18, 1943, 6.00am–6.00pm, 12 hours at 5½d per hour.' My dad was a fitter's mate. What the fitter fitted, or how my father assisted him, or how I, aged four and three-quarters (the fitter's mate's mate), assisted *him* that far-off Sunday at the height of World War II, I cannot for the life of me recall. My dad for much of my childhood was the invisible man. A fitter's mate, a labourer really, his hourly pay so pitifully low, he needed all the overtime there was to make a living wage. He'd leave the house when I was asleep and return when I was asleep. From his point of view, I was the invisible boy.

I try, even so, to capture some memories, some details of that tantalizing day (drop the bucket down) when I was with my dad. Did I have little overalls on? A knapsack, maybe? Bottle of cold tea, like Dad's, with a rolled-up paper stopper in its neck (and haul it up)? Were we picked up in the works van? The fitter's van? Did I, perhaps . . . (empty).

I have in my possession, found among my mother's effects in 1987, a Prudential Assurance policy: Whole Life Assurance on Life of Another for Funeral Expenses. It goes on:

9

Whereas a proposal has been made by the person named in the schedule [my mother] to effect an assurance upon the life of the child named in the said schedule [me]. Age next birthday of the child stated at ONE years. Sum Assured Payable At Death Subject To The Conditions Indorsed hereon:

£6 if the child dies under age 3.
£10   do.   do.   at or after age 3 and under age 6.
£15   do.   do.   at or after age 6.
Amount of weekly premium. ONE PENNY.

And again I lower the bucket down for the child, age stated at ONE years. Nothing. What a pity. What a shame that we're unable – any of us really – to recover, draw up, those baby months, weeks, hours, when we were aliens on the Earth, drinking its milk for the first time, feeling its soft wool, smelling its fatherly and motherly skins, howling at it. Or later, going with our father for twelve whole hours, or even more with the journey time, to work with him at 5½d an hour, all day on a Sunday. In the war. When did you last see your father? When did you first see him?

Dad was a smoker, all men were in those days. He was a Woodbine man, who would occasionally at my request smoke Turf so I could collect the cigarette cards. It killed him, of course, when I was seventeen and he was fifty-five. The thing is, I am not greedy. It need not be a bucket, an eggcup would do, a spoon, an eye-dropper. Something, at least, a little more than an oblong scrap of paper with sepia writing on it.

The Mangle

In the steamy wash house
My mother's face is pink
As she wrestles with dad's overalls
In the soap-suddy sink.

The overalls don't like it
I see them fighting back
Mum wrings their arms and legs out
The water turns quite black.

My mother's arms are mighty
Her shoulders rise and fall
The scrubbing brush is in her hand
And green soap conquers all.

The mangle's my opponent
It lifts me off my feet
It takes the total weight of me
To mangle up a sheet.

Two heavy wooden rollers
Cogs like a giant clock
A handle for the turning.
Sheet, shirt or sock

Goes squelching in on one side
Comes flattened out the other
I fling that handle high and wide
And help my boiling mother.

With puny muscles all geared up
My strength is that of ten
We feed the overalls to their doom
And feed them in again.

The battle's almost over
The vanquished washing lies
In a woven wooden basket
The mangle creaks and sighs.

A smell of soot from the boiler
Sweat on my youthful nose
Steam on mother's glasses
A pile of flattened clothes.

The wash house stands deserted
As silent as the grave
The mangle, damp and dripping
A monster in a cave.

While elsewhere in the windy yard
Pegged out and looking fine
Dad's resurrected overalls
Are dancing on the line.

The Worm Bank

The world was at my feet when I was a little boy. I could squat down so easily to see it. And when you are little, you see the little. I was my own microscope: the chestnut-coloured, fine and furry coat of a caterpillar, the creamy dust of a butterfly's wing that came away on your fingers, leaving a delicate tracery – like an old leaf – exposed; the tiniest transparent fish in the shallow margins of the park pond; the water boatman boating, the rapid centipede revealed beneath a house brick, scuttling for cover; slow unflappable woodlice; ladybirds, spiders, snails.

I spent some time, happy half-hours, in the gutter in those days, or near it – the rainwater close up, like a river in spate – sailing cigarette packets, matchsticks, paper boats. And my eyes so sharp and my nose so keen. The smell of tar, still soft at the edges of a freshly made-up road. You could take it and roll it into a little ball and not have it stick to you. The smell of dirt, pond water, grass. Grass stains on your elbows and knees. A grub revealed in the core of an apple, fleas jumping about in Dinah's coat. A daddy-long-legs drowning in a toilet. Worms on hooks. Yes, worms. (And my ears so . . . pricked up.) I remember The Worm Bank.

The Worm Bank was a compost heap in the park, added to from time to time by the park gardeners. A secret, humid place, a tropical bubble surrounded by rhododendron bushes. It was beloved by boys and fishermen, home to a particular breed of thin red worm (beloved by fish). I was there helping another even littler boy collecting worms for his fisherman dad. Albert, his digging spoon in hand, was down on his haunches. Of a sudden, he paused in his work and cocked his head on one side, like a bird.

'Listen,' he said. 'Y'can hear 'em.'

I may have supposed he was pulling my leg, but paused then in *my* work and listened. And there it was, the faintest, tiniest sound, a dry rustling in the leaf mould. Worms on the move.

Bluebells and Yellowhammers

There's an event that I remember, half-remember, mis-remember? I've looked at a map, matched up the history and the topography of it: a couple of hills, two or three miles, seven or eight kids. There was a pram, I'm pretty sure, and a probable baby. It was May, had to be May, early June at the latest, and there were bluebells, definitely bluebells, that was the whole point. Bluebells, bluebells, all the way, a holy grail of them. And yellowhammers.

We would have gathered in the morning after breakfast (and jobs). Me and Brian, say, or Trevor, Trevor's little brother Malky, Spencer, possibly, Graham Glew, perhaps. Pat and Maureen, two popular girls – they'd have had charge of the pram – and a baby, a cousin of Pat's or a neighbour's child. Provisioned by our mothers, sugar sandwiches and Tizer, a few if-we-were-lucky sweets. Spanish root and liquorice. Bottles of water. Sticks of rhubarb.

This is where we'd go. Up Rood End Road, past the Mer-rivale, up Barnford Hill, through Barnford Park – in and out of it – down a path between high hedges, across a field, across the dual-carriagewayed New Wolverhampton Road, around the edge of Brandhall golf course – away from the smoke and noise of the town (out from under it) – up a path beside more hedges, down a dip and round and on and into . . . Bluebell Wood.

It took a day, a whole day there and back, of elastic time, the rise and fall of the sun, eating and drinking, talking and shoving, peeing in the bushes, soothing our nettle-stung legs with dock leaves. There was the colour of the floor of the woods (our reason for coming), a blue mist hovering, which we disrupted somewhat with bunches of instantly wilted bluebells, gifts for our mothers, trophies, carried off home. Yes, loaded on to the pram most likely. And the air was heavy and drugged, and so were we.

But wasn't there a stile somewhere we had to cross? A lumpy, rutted path around a field? A tank trap for a pram? Maybe so. All the same, there was a pram, a baby carriage come to that. Coach-built! And a baby, a wondrously placid baby – accommodating – with his or her own wondrous provisions: sweet milk, orange juice, rusks. A child-raised baby. Yes, we will retain the baby, not give him up for the world.

And the yellowhammers? They were in those final hedges, nests of them, with their exquisitely scribbled-on eggs, which I, definitely, and Brian or Trevor, probably, took, carried home, pierced with a pin, blew, labelled and transferred at the last into another nest of fluffed-out cotton wool. In a shoebox.

But the thing is, not the bluebells or the yellowhammers (so much for a title) or the unlikely pram even. The thing is: how did we know where to go? And so unerringly. Our ages were ten and nine and nine, and eight and six, say, five, possibly . . . and a baby. I only remember going once. Nobody, as I recall, led the way. We simply went. It seems to me now we were like wildebeest or spawning salmon. No maps or adult guidance, just a current of prior knowledge flowing through us, or printed in us, like the lettering in a stick of rock.

And that's it, maybe. I might only remember going once, but I'd been before, I bet, as a four-year-old, or the baby even, in the pram. Our parents, uncles, cousins, grandparents would have made the trip in earlier times, before the road was a dual carriageway, before the park was a park, before the golf course was ever dreamed of.

Well, the golf course has shrunk now, encroached upon by houses, the Merrivale is boarded up, the New Wolverhampton Road showing its age. But is the trail still there? Did the baby on his own two feet go again? Did *his* baby? And might a ghostly tribe of shaven-headed boys and pig-tailed girls come meandering (yet purposefully) along through people's gardens, backyards, hallways, once a year in May or early June, along the golf-course streets

with sections of surviving hedgerows (no yellowhammers).
A ghostly tribe plus pram exercising, quite rightfully, their
right of way?

Old Soap

Begin at the beginning
Old soap in a cup
Hot water from the kettle
And a spoon to stir it up.

A soup of soap, slimy and green, like frogspawn, like snot.
A clay pipe that, more often than not, produced when blown
a myriad of tiny bubbles and a noise like a clucking hen. It
was difficult to isolate one bubble and enlarge it. Better a
ring of wire, like half a pair of glasses. (The old soap, its sharp
incisions, its name, its decorations, worn away. The old cup,
chipped, no handle, demoted.) Then, out of the slime – a

butterfly from its chrysalis – a larger bubble, wobbly and iridescent. Or perhaps, when you are very little, someone else is blowing them, casting them adrift for you to chase across the grimy yard, between the houses and the wash houses, the washing lines and dustbins. Yes, I see it now, those floating bubbles, some caught and splattered between my chubby hands, others escaping, rising, losing their mirrored sheen, becoming at the last mere empty circles in the air. Above the wash-house roofs and upturned faces. And going (end at the end), an instantaneous annihilation. Pop.

Brierley Hill

Once a month on a Sunday
When the town was slow and still
I went with my mournful mother
On a bus to Brierley Hill.

I had my Sunday suit on
And knew I must behave
As we rode on the upper deck
To Auntie Mabel's grave.

The whole world died on Sundays
Back then as I recall
Shops shuttered, factories dumb
You could not kick a ball.

We carried a bunch of flowers
Chrysanths, I remember the smell
A pair of scissors to cut the stalks
Some cleaning cloths as well.

The cemetery was small and high
You could see halfway to Clent
Gravestones angled like giant teeth
Discoloured and bent.

Mum did a bit of weeding
Removed dead flowers from the pot
The marble pot (named Mabel)
Gone but not forgot.

My job was to fetch the water
And carry it up to the grave
And not put my hands in my pockets
Or whistle, or misbehave.

But the thing I really remember
Is the squealing that filled the air
From Marsh & Baxter's factory
And the pigs imprisoned there.

Yes, the whole world died on Sundays
And the pigs they were not dumb
They squealed for their lives disappearing
And the sausages they'd become.

It surely did upset me
Scare me, that echoing sound
Far worse than the lurching gravestones
Or the bodies underground.

I was glad when we departed
And hurried off down the hill
And caught the bus back to Oldbury
Where the town was slow and still.

The Clothes Horse

A wooden frame like a folded fence
Or a windbreak, three feet high
It stands in the kitchen on winter nights
With the washing spread out to dry.

And into that steamy tent I creep
And under that 60-watt sun
I spy on the enemy's forces
And pick them off with my gun.

My hair's slicked flat, my cheeks are pink
My face has an apple's shine
The rest of the room is Mum and Dad's
But the clothes-horse space is mine.

And under these billowing sheets I sail
Over those rag-rug waves
To islands of parrots and pirates
Palm trees and treasure caves.

My dad sits painting a soldier
My mum sits darning a sock
The fire shuffles down in the fireplace
Time ticks by in the clock.

And I sit tight in the clothes horse
Where the socks and the palm trees sway
Directing my soldiers and shipmates
Hard at work at my play.

The radio talks in the corner
Just William, *ITMA*, news
Mum pours tea from the teapot
Dad cleans a pair of shoes.

A wooden frame like a folded fence
Or a deckchair on its side
With laundered flags a-fluttering
And room for a boy to hide.

The air has a soapyish flavour
A freshly ironed smell
While our lives shuffle down in the kitchen
I remember the embers . . . well.

I do remember the clothes horse, almost more than any
other domestic item from my childhood (except, possibly,
the mangle). I could have called this whole book *The Clothes
Horse*, had I not used the title already for a previous collec-
tion of stories. When Jessica was small, she once asked Janet
what a 'jackpot' was. She had heard it on the radio. I came
in in the middle of their conversation and contributed.

Yes, well, y'see, there was this giant who had a problem
with boys named Jack. They were forever creeping up to

his house, hiding behind the milk bottles, getting into his slippers, pestering his wife. So, finally, the exasperated giant had an idea. He got a big pot and put it in the kitchen next to the fridge. After that, whenever he or his wife or their small (fourteen-foot) son came upon a Jack, they'd pick him up and drop him into the pot. Each evening the giant would stroll down the garden and empty the pot at the far end, which from the Jacks' point of view was about fifteen miles away.

Jessica appeared content with this explanation. I, for my part, was (briefly) overjoyed with it. Look what I had stumbled on! The language itself was full to overflowing with words and phrases like *The Jack Pot* that contained, had folded up within them so to speak, entire stories. *Night Train, Fire Escape, No Man's Land, Car Park, The Shadow Chancellor.* It was an oil well, a gold mine. I could write one a week for years. Well, in the finish I wrote, let's see, all told a dozen or more, and published ten. And the first of them, inevitably I now feel, was:

THE CLOTHES HORSE

Once upon a time a magician made a horse out of clothes. He used two pairs of trousers for the legs, two pairs of shoes for the feet, a mac for the back and a tie for the tail. The head was made from a large sock, with buttons for eyes and a painted mouth. The magician cheated a little with the ears, however. They were cut out of felt and sewn on.

Well, the truth is this horse didn't look too much like a horse, when you got close to him, which I suppose was only to be expected. All the same, he had been put together by a magician, and could therefore gallop and neigh and eat his bag of oats with the best of them.

For a time the horse found himself a job pulling a milkman's cart; this was in the old days, before they had milk-floats. But he soon got bored with this and ran away (galloped away, I should say). The milkman didn't mind too much, however. He was bored with being a milkman. And the magician wasn't bothered either. He was occupied just then making a cat out of bottle tops.

Well, the horse ran away, and – to cut a long story short (or a short one shorter) – had his trousers stolen by a couple of tramps whose own trousers had worn out. His mac was taken by a little girl who wanted to make a tent with it. His tie was 'borrowed' by a man who couldn't get into a restaurant unless he was

31

wearing one; and his sock was removed by another man (with a wooden leg) who was getting married.

Anyway, by this time there was not too much left of the horse. (There isn't too much left of the story either.) For a little while he did try walking around (or trotting, I should say) in just his shoes. But he only felt silly doing this, and besides it often scared people (dogs, too) to see four shoes coming down the road with nobody in them. They thought it was a ghost – no, two ghosts!

So, finally, one bright and sunny morning the horse stepped out of his shoes and completely disappeared. Then he thought to himself: This must be the end of me! And it was.

Well, perhaps not entirely the end, if the truth be known. He was still there after all; you just couldn't see him. Anyway, what happened later (this is really another story, but I will tell it all the same), what happened later was this: The horse went back to haunt the magician and play tricks on the bottle-top cat. And after that he had the clever idea of stealing washing. He stole two pairs of pyjama bottoms, a couple of blankets, another sock, a sun hat ... and so on. Finally, so I've heard, he got a job on the stage – pantomimes, mostly. Perhaps you have seen him. Of course, some people think he is really just two men dressed up as a horse. There again, you and I know better, don't we? *

33

* *The Clothes Horse and Other Stories* (1987).

The Depths of the Painting

I can see it from where I sit. It is a proper painting – in a frame. An old man on a horse. A little girl and a little boy also on the horse. The old man has a sword. There are some ducks – and reeds – and a river. The little girl looks worried. The little boy looks worrieder.

He is a knight, Miss Palmer says. Sir Isumbras. He is saving the children. The picture is *Sir Isumbras at the Ford*, which is a shallow part of the river (not a car), Miss Palmer says, where you may cross.

I cross. I leave my seat and cross. And enter the picture. The ducks fly up, the reeds bend, the water splashes. The fish . . . the horse. We need another horse; four on a horse is too many. A pony, a pony like Ice-cream Jack's, or I could have a bike. I could have armour, golden like Sir Isumbras's. And a sword.

I made a sword once from a chestnut paling and the lid of a powdered-milk tin. I could use that. My pony's name is . . . Billy.

> Where the pools are bright and deep
> Where the grey trout lies asleep
> Up the river and over the lea
> That's the way for Billy and me.

I learnt this poem for Recitation. In my report it says: 'Recitation – marks out of 20 – 19; position in class – 7'. It also says: 'Writing – 14 out of 20, position in class 41; Craft – 9 out of 20, position in class 51'.

I help Sir Isumbras. He gives me jobs. I can be the lookout, or I can gallop off and fetch things. On the other side of the river or round a bend there will be a castle. I can gallop off there with a message. Billy and me. Miss Palmer is speaking. Allan, she says. And asks me something. Now I am worried. I need Sir Isumbras to save me too. I shrivel in my seat. Hands raised up, around me and against me. What's the answer? What's the answer? What's the question? I come out of the picture.

'Allan could do much better,' Miss Palmer writes in my school report (for the half-year ending December 1946). 'He is most inattentive and dreamy at times.'

I am not inattentive. I am attentive. For instance, now, aeons later (for the half-year ending December 2011), I attentively google Sir Isumbras and see him for the first time in sixty-five years. I observe now that *he* looks worried. (It's a big responsibility, taking care of children. My child is thirty-two; my stepchildren, twenty-six and twenty.) I google *Sir Isumbras at the Ford* by Sir John Everett Millais (1829–96). The girl is bigger than I remembered, the boy has a bundle of sticks on his back. There are no ducks; they must have flown in from the park, or I made them up. No evidence either of my presence in the picture, my passage through it, up the river and over the ford. No telltale pony's hoof prints or home-made sword abandoned in the reeds. But a sleeping trout, perhaps, who knows, down there in the painting's hidden depths.

The Pillowcase

Christmas came in a pillowcase. How old was I when I first knew what to do? Three, four? My main duty was to endure the passage of time. How long was the day before Christmas Eve? How long was Christmas Eve itself? Time, of course, as we all learn, accelerates with life, rushes off with us at the end. But it does so from a standing start. Three-year-olds creep like snails through their days. Baby time is geological.

Our house (on Cemetery Road), two down, three up, outside lavatory and wash house, had no heating in its upstairs rooms. There was a chilly dampness there. On winter nights my mother put a hot shelf from the oven wrapped in a towel in my bed to warm it up. It was at first too hot to rest my feet on. The bedroom curtains were thin, light seeped in from the street. There was a rag rug on the floor, shiny lino.

So . . . I would get up and creep on to the landing, far too early. Sounds from the kitchen below: the wireless, voices, clattering cups. I'd return to bed, sleep and wake again. The hot plate is cold, the lino cold, the street lamp out, the darkness pitch. And yet . . . there, out on the landing, glowing as if from an inner source of light, is the pillowcase. I drag it back into the room, heave it on to the bed. What time is it? Three o'clock, three-thirty, four? I put the light on and unwrap my treasures: a Bakelite cowboy on a horse, a wind-up car, model soldiers – shop-bought, perhaps, or home-made – a kit for making cotton-reel tanks, a box of games: Ludo, Snakes and Ladders. No books, as I recall. Sweets and nuts. An orange.

I can remember, from out of those slow-moving times, particular and special gifts. A mouth organ in its own red lacquered box lined with green velvet. A toy fort complete with matchstick-firing cannon. A miniature gramophone with matching records: *Snow White and the Seven Dwarfs*, 'Some day my prince will come' . . . 'Heigh-ho, heigh-ho!' The enduring memory, though, and the source of this short piece, is none of these, or their unwrapping even. No, it's that first glimpse on the landing, the mysterious shape, and all my little heart and soul swept up, consumed, in the discovery of it.

Trapdoors in the Grass

My head in a towel, my wet hair being dried. The barber is as old as me, or thereabouts. He dries my hair the way my mother did, but not so roughly. He even dries inside my ears as she did. When I was little, the towel enveloped me. Tin bath in front of the fire, pyjamas warming on the oven door, soap in a cup.

My mother was a cleaner, of offices and other people's houses and me. She did a thorough job, beating back the tide of dirt that ever sought to claim her precious son. Screwing one corner of the skinny towel into my ears, like a bradawl.

My mother's cleaning jobs opened up new worlds for us: posher houses, gardens, garages. The daughter of one family she cleaned for, Cecilia her name was, Cecilia, such a flowing, such a romantic name; aristocratic. Ce-ci-li-a. And her brother was my age and size. Now and then I'd inherit one of his unwanted but still-wearable shirts, thin pretty stripes, or a jumper of the softest wool. Otherwise my jumpers were home-made, hand-knitted by my mum or Auntie Mabel. My hands manacled, yes, handcuffed by the skeins of Auntie Mabel's wool.

Another posh person was Mr Griffin, the insurance man (collar and tie, waistcoat, briefcase), calling once a week to collect his money, accumulating his heavy load of shillings, sixpences and pennies. The smoke from his pipe often arrived before he did. He had a bald head with a semicircular fringe of hair, like my present barber, and for that matter his two barber sons, here now at their respective chairs, left and left again of their father. A bald trio of barbers . . . my head in a towel . . . the memorable aroma of Mr Griffin's pipe.

When my mother was old and I was middle-aged, I would visit her in her council bungalow high up on the Rounds Green Hills. She would stand behind me (like the barber now) as I sat in a chair and tap lightly with her knuckles on the top of my head, sounding me out like a coconut or a boiled egg. 'Where's it all come from then?' she'd ask. Meaning all those children's books I was writing. Good, bad or indifferent they may have been, but there were a lot of them. It was a puzzle to her, how I had turned out. And she'd pretend to open me up, lift my lid, look inside.

There's a flash of light, caught on a windscreen in the street outside, bouncing about in the barber's mirror, fractured in its bevelled edges, rainbowed. The shop-window lettering, reversed and reversed again in the mirror, out of sense and back into it.

And I recall the trapdoors in the grass. In the park. Cut with Billy Harold's penknife, three sides and the fourth for a hinge. Lift the lid and look inside. A little cavity, treasures hidden – toy soldier, marble, penny – and returned to later, rediscovered. I bet we lost a few things, though, forgot their whereabouts. There again, the park is still there with its descendant grass. I could go back and look.

Mr Cotterill

The man who cuts my hair
He makes me sweat
He takes his tea in a shaving mug
And smokes a cigarette.

He waves his clippers all about
Talks football with the men
Sat waiting – fags and overalls –
In Cotterill's smoking den.

I kneel up in the chair
He wraps me in a sheet
And cuts off half my hair
It gathers at his feet.

He wears peculiar glasses
A knitted Albion scarf
His crazy clippers roaring in
To clip the other half.

I am a big boy now
(My mother tells me so)
But my head is getting smaller
And my mouth's a frightened 'o'.

I watch him in the mirror
As his clippers take their toll
His eyes swim out of focus
Like blue fish in a bowl.

The man who cuts my hair
He makes me quake
He drinks his tea with a slurping noise
And eats a Jaffa Cake.

I dream sometimes of haircuts
I'm in a mighty chair
In a forest full of scissors
In a clearing full of hair.

In a palace full of money
In a garden full of clothes
With a maid and one big barber . . .
Who snips off my nose.

Apples of Old

They don't make apples like they did when I was a boy. Or breakfasts, bacon still flinching from the slicer, spiteful eggs spitting in the pan. Bread does not arrive still hot on the doorstep with its curve of crust all ready to be torn off, inverted like a boat or barge and filled with butter. The butter, almost green at the edges, with a delicious hint of sourness in its taste. They don't make butter like they did. Or beer.

When I became a man and travelled, I'd seek out that taste of beer my father sometimes let me have: bitter, smelly, unpleasant really, but highly interesting when you are six or seven. On holidays I'd track down obscure CAMRA ales, ever hoping to be reacquainted with my father's beer. For years I searched and supped until it dawned on me; the beer I sought was gone for good. Even if some cunning brewer brewed it up – hops, water, yeast – exactly as it was, I would not taste it. The taste was a contract, a particular deal between that beer and my mouth, my young six-year-old mouth, likewise gone for good.

Yes, like passing trains, I guess, the world goes one way and we, though gazing backwards, go the other.

Sunlight

The ever-increasing variety of the town's industries augurs well for the future prosperity of Oldbury. Besides the wide range of its hardware output, from edge-tools to bicycle frames, and of its chemicals, from alkali to phosphorus, it produces blue bricks and cardboard boxes, tar, jam, and pale ale, immense engine boilers and delicate surgical dressings, and a catalogue of other manufactures equally strange in their diversity to say nothing of the railway carriages and the canal barges by which they may be expeditiously carried away.

Oldbury and Round About,
Frederick William Hackwood (1915)

The sun shone down on Oldbury
When I was growing up
Under the rusty Rounds Green Hills
In a hot and sulphurous cup.

Corrugated-iron roofs
Corroded and oily ground
Forty-five factory chimneys to count
Without even turning round.

Accles & Pollock, Danks's
Chance & Hunt, The Brades
Used up the air of Oldbury
As they followed their various trades.

A layer of low commercial smoke
A lid upon the town
Shut out the feeble fabled sky
Kept us from turning brown.

Such little mushroomed kids we were
Our knees so nearly white
You'd spot us halfway up the street
In the middle of the night.

Yet everyone had his chimney
Kindling, coal or coke
Bonfires bloomed in gardens
Lives went up in smoke.

Dads cloth-capped and muffled
Dads with dogs in the park
Coughing their way to the factories
Puffing their fags in the dark.

A town of arsonists, you'd say
Combusting our desires
Even the mothers sooted their sheets
With their very own wash-house fires.

Then once a year in August
We'd quit the town at a run
And catch the train to the seaside
And lie down and worship the sun.

And come back burnt to a cinder
As red as a post-office brick
Back to our blanket of Oldbury smoke
And under it, quiet and quick.

It was our town, all said and done
Our home through thick and thin
The sun shone down on Oldbury, yes
But we wouldn't let it in.

Treading the Boilers

Some memories I have of the most convincing kind that are not my own. I'm in a rowing boat on a river with my mother and father. A tiny little boy. The rowing boat, as we prepare to disembark, tips up. All of us then in the water. 'Save Allan!' my mother cries. 'Save him! Save him!' (i.e. not her). My father – an excellent swimmer, who as a boy had dived for pennies thrown by sailors off Tynemouth docks – saves us both. But it's my mother's memory not mine I'm remembering, and my father's, diving for pennies, told to me when I was little, less little, and eventually not so little at all. Memories I've adopted, memories tailored for me by my parents, like a suit of clothes. Bespoke.

Or I'm on my tricycle in the yard behind our house in Birchfield Lane. An air-raid shelter has been dismantled (or bombed) and lies half-buried in a hole or crater. So down I tumble. I scrape my knees, lose a tooth, get a nasty cut from a jutting edge of corrugated iron. But again it's my mother and others, aunties and such, who store the memory up and read it back to me in later times, rehearse me in it until I'm word perfect. Though in this case there is corroboration of a sort: a small white scar on the inside of my wrist that did not finally fade till I was forty.

And then there was Treading the Boilers. I cherished this memory so much that in the finish I worked it up and put it into a story.

On Monday morning in assembly Mr Reynolds talked to the whole school about boys playing on bomb sites, boys trespassing in Messrs Danks's factory yard and storage areas, nits, Jesus and the Coronation Cup.

A boy named Horace Crumpton had fallen and dislocated his shoulder while fooling around in a derelict house. Mr Reynolds felt sure we could learn a lesson from him. Horace took a bow, embarrassed and pleased with himself, arm in a sling. Other boys, so far unidentified, had been chased out of Danks's on Saturday night by the watchman. It was Amos and his lot treading the boilers again, but Mr Reynolds was not to know this. He was sick and tired of getting phone calls to his home, he said, and promised retribution.

And then, a day or so later . . .

Patrick, it turned out, had been one of the gang of boys – organized by Amos – who under the cover of fog and darkness had last night revisited Danks's. Treading the boilers involved a dozen or so boys getting inside a boiler and walking in unison, causing it to roll. For some boys, notably Amos, this was an addictive experience. Danks's manufactured boilers of all sizes, used in ships and so on. They stored them in a nearby field. The story goes that the first time boys ever worked this trick, the watchman had a heart attack. There was this huge red-oxidized cylinder rolling off all by itself in the moonlight.[*]

In the moonlight, yes – all by itself. What a scene! I can picture it – hologram it – even now. Danks's was there, and Danks's boilers in a fenced-off field, and the gang of boys inside the boiler, they were there. And I . . . was not there. Not me. Never. It was Donald – Donald, my cousin. He was there. Yet somehow down the years I have been pulled into Donald's memory, or insinuated my way into it, absorbing all the while its atmosphere, its romance. I remember it now better than Donald himself. The factory-lit sky, the moon, half in, half out of the clouds, so that the watch-man's revelation has a sudden, illuminated, religious almost, quality to it. The watchman's wavering torch, his croaky voice, the wet grass, the running off and scrambling under a gap in the fence, gasping at last, breath smoking in the air, a congregation of little boys gathering to rehearse *their*

[*] *The Boyhood of Burglar Bill* (2006).

memories, no doubt, beneath a street lamp. It is a memory. Oh yes, it is a memory all right, and – sorry, Don – it's mine.

Child Watching

I am on a stage in a great big hall, called Bingley Hall. A big boy in a beard is lifting me on to a table. I am wearing a sort of blanket nightshirt with coloured stripes. It hangs down to my ankles. My face and hands and feet are painted brown with some cocoa-smelling stuff. My real clothes, socks and shoes, are backstage in the cloakroom. My brand-new blazer is there. It is a green one with brass buttons.

The big boy in the beard is listening. God is speaking to him. His loud voice fills the hall. It will be my turn soon. I must remember what to say. And speak up. The big boy in the beard is staring at me now. A drip of sweat is shining on his nose. He has a knife.

Forty years later, another hall. I'm standing at the back watching an infant assembly. Jessica's class is performing a series of short scenes and tableaux on the subject of 'Time'. Jessica has a major role as the little old lady. I am, of course, transfixed, though not so much that I cannot see this open goal before me; a poem on a plate. Other parents are snapping away with their cameras. I scribble some notes and hurry home to my shed.

THE INFANTS DO AN ASSEMBLY
ABOUT TIME

The infants
Do an assembly
About Time.

It has the past,
The present
And the future in it;
The seasons,
A digital watch,
And a six-year-old
Little old lady.

She gets her six-year-old
Family up
And directs them
Through the twenty-four hours
Of the day:

Out of bed
And – shortly after –
Back into it.
(Life does not stand still
In infant assemblies.)

The whole thing
Lasts for fifteen minutes.
Next week (space permitting):
Space.*

And the question is, when did I leave the stage and join the audience? I was for a time in my twenties and early thirties a teacher. I remember a boy in my first class, Glen Brakes his name was. A mild, no-trouble-to-anybody sort of boy. On one occasion, and before he got to know me,

*Heard it in the Playground (1989).

my gaze fell on him in the classroom. He had acquired a feather and was dreamily stroking his own nose and mouth with it, and inside his ear. Glen had a pleasant face. He resembled Stan Laurel (of Laurel and Hardy). Well, Laurel and Hardy both would have admired Glen's subsequent bit of mime when caught in the teacher's (unintended) searchlight glare. He juggled with the feather, gazed at it in disbelief. Is this a feather that I see before me? Who's put this feather, forced this feather into my unwilling hand? When I have work to do.

Sometimes at playtime through the staff-room window I would see a little infant haring by, take a tumble. He or she, briefly shocked, would scramble up and look around. A lower lip would tremble, a frown. Then came the fork in the road. If the fall had gone unnoticed, the child would, like as not, dust himself down and go haring off again. But if the dinner lady, say, or teacher on duty witnessed the event and caught *his* eye ... Then, of course, the warmth of her sympathy, like a poultice with a bee sting, would draw his hot tears out.

There again, teachers for the most part mostly observe children, wouldn't you say? In my case I did not start *watching* them with any serious intent until Jessica was born.

*

56

Bingley Hall is very big and full of people. They stretch away into the darkness. My Sunday School is there, and all the other Sunday Schools, and Sunday School teachers, and the mums and dads, and the aunties and uncles, grandmas and grandpas. We are doing a pageant. Oh yes, and there's a balcony full of people. It is very hot in Bingley Hall. My cocoa colouring is getting streaky. It rubs off on to my stripy shirt, though I am lying on the table as still as ever I can. Hot lights shine down on to the stage. God has nearly finished, I think. I listen out for my cue.

A couple of years ago in the town where I now live, on the main shopping street, I saw a woman with two boys. The boys were five, perhaps, and three. They were identically dressed in what appeared to be home-made one-piece garments, like workmen's overalls, with three-quarter-length trouser legs and straps over the shoulders. The material was striped and stiff; there was a good deal of orange in it. They looked like a pair of little walking deckchairs.

I was hypnotized by them, stepped into a doorway to see them pass and watched them out of sight. And it occurred to me later, suppose someone had been watching *me*; the trouble I might have been in. The end of a career. Thirty years ago you could watch children, talk to them even on occasion, in public places. For instance, recollect – as I am sure you can – the volcanic, all-encompassing turmoil and distress in the tiny heart of a tiny person in Sainsbury's, say. Witness the brick-red face, hair damply plastered to the head, flailing arms and legs. Who would not wish to comfort someone in a state like that? Crouch down, lean in, offer distractions, sympathize. But it is almost, well almost almost, too risky now. These days I mostly share my sociable remarks with dogs. Dogs you can talk to, and the owners, of course, invariably appreciate it.

Meanwhile, back at Bingley Hall, high drama. God finally shuts up. The big boy in the beard says something. I sit up on the table and shout my lines. An organ plays. There is an organ in Bingley Hall. It is so big and loud you can feel it (hear it!) through the soles of your feet. The pageant now is nearly over. We all come back on stage, hundreds of us, for a final song. 'Jesus Wants Me for a Sunbeam', it might have been. Everybody claps. The clapping is louder even than the organ.

Now we are all backstage having our faces wiped clean of the cocoa stuff. I am getting dressed when suddenly dread fills me up. I cannot find my blazer. My brand-new, bought-specially-for-the-occasion blazer. It has gone. Some sinner has pinched it! Tears flood up into my eyes. I loved my lovely day-old blazer. The shine of its buttons, the green of its cloth, the brand-new smell of it. And what will I tell my mother? What *will* I tell her? She'll murder me for sure.

It was a bad end to the day, a disastrous end. Oh yes, God saved me, Isaac, from my father Abraham's knife – though it was cardboard – but he never saved my blazer, did he? No, too busy shouting his head off up in Bingley Hall.

The Boat

My mum came back from Birmingham
Removed her hat and coat
Kicked off her shoes and sighed and said
'I nearly bought you a boat.'

I knew this boat, I'd seen it
In a shop on Colmore Row
A clockwork tin-toy steamer
Plus box: Chad Valley & Co.

I knew this boat, its painted tin
Its funnel with a key
Its painted passengers, its flags
It was the boat for me.

So all I heard was boat and bought
(The clock in the kitchen stopped)
I never heard the nearly
Until the penny dropped.

Mum made herself a cup of tea
And buttered me a scone
And spoke of Auntie Elsie's legs
And switched the wireless on.

Some other boats I know I had
A paddle boat, a yacht
An Airfix model landing craft
All more or less forgot –

Like paper boats in the gutter
Soon swirling down the drain –
Only that steadfast nearly boat
Sails in my memory, plain.

The prettiest, shiniest never gift
Just destined to become
The present most treasured from the past
From my old mum. Thanks, Mum.

Dad's Army

My dad makes little soldiers
In moulds with molten lead
With caps and guns and bayonets
And paints them green and red

And blue and black and silver
They line up in a row
With hair and eyes and eyebrows
Each one of them just so.

My dad works as a labourer
His hands are seamed with grime
And cracked and cut and calloused
And no amount of time

Spent scrubbing in the wash house
Or soaking in the sink
Can shift that dirt away
Though the water's black as ink.

The bosses in Dad's factory
Don't notice him, I'll bet
No suit - no tie - no title
He's easy to forget.

But back at home it's different
Who's bothered with a suit?
For me, I love Dad's army
And the soldiers - they salute.

Territory

We alight at Oldbury, in Worcestershire, a place of smother amid smother, and, on leaving the station, can count seventy-nine furnace and factory chimneys without turning round, all of which pour forth their cloudy contributions, varied by the blue and yellow smoke of copper works, while noises resound afar.

All Round the Wrekin, Walter White (1860)

Oldbury was the town I grew up in, but the bit of Oldbury I really grew up in was Rood End, and the bit of Rood End I really grew up in - the territory of my childhood - was The Park, The Allotments and The Cemetery. The cemetery backed on to the park, and the park and the cemetery backed on to the allotments, and the allotments backed on to them. It was The World.

I climbed trees in the park and saw a kingfisher in the allotments. A brook flowed from the park into and between the cemetery and the allotments. I dug up potatoes on the allotments that were not mine, pinched peas in the pod, carrots. I saw a ghost in the boathouse, dug for worms in The Worm Bank that, you might reasonably suppose, had

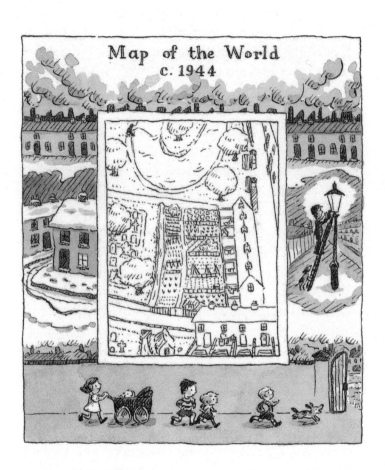

Map of the World
c. 1944

wormed their way in under the fence from the cemetery, where they worked. I climbed the, albeit smaller, trees in the cemetery, looking for nests; read about death (and resurrection) there:

Until the Day Breaks
Resting Where No Shadows Fall
Safe in the Arms of Jesus
Be Ye Also Ready.

Truth is, you needed to be ready in those days, for the freedoms we enjoyed came at a price: 'Five-year-old Cedric Harry Cooke after bird nesting with his brother Anthony was found dead in six feet of water in a pool at Darbys Hill quarry. Police gave artificial respiration in vain. The facts have been reported to the coroner', *Oldbury Weekly News*.

Our parents let us go. They let us go, back then in Oldbury, well Rood End, well . . . round by us. And poor Cedric Harry, or the boy who drowned in Tipton Canal with his foot jammed in a submerged tangle of bedsprings, or the boy who fell through the floor of a derelict house on to his head, paid the price.

Some of it was our own fault. We evaded, with no great difficulty, the park-keepers, allotment holders, grave-diggers who might otherwise have steered us to a safer path. We infiltrated that little and enormous world, ducking low and out of sight, guerrillas camouflaged as children.

Mr and Mrs Cooke could have saved their errant son by keeping him close, keeping him in, safe from motorbikes and buses, bombed-out buildings, marlholes and spiked railings, dangerous dogs . . . and men. Safe too, of course, from sticklebacks, bluebells and yellowhammers, wind and rain.

This piece is getting away from me. I had not intended to follow young Cedric quite so far. It's supposed to be about territory. I took a wrong turning back there, round about 'Be Ye Also Ready'. Hm . . . let's try again, one more paragraph at least.

Territory: this patch of ground in which I am forever planted and to which, two or three times a year, I return. I visit my cousins up on the Rounds Green Hills, have a pint or two in The Lamp or The Waggon and Horses. The park has shrunk, the boathouse (a ghost itself) long since demolished, the allotments a billowing sea of poly tunnels. But the cemetery endures more or less as it ever was. Death and decay, it seems, have passed it by. I carry flowers to my parents' grave, a pair of scissors to cut the stalks, J Cloth to wipe the gravestone, plastic bottle of water. Yes, the grave

(George Henry and Elizabeth Mary) is there. You could find it, if you cared to, down at the bottom end, away from the park on the railway side, with a school and its playground beyond. Often then on such occasions I hear, as I tidy the grave and arrange the flowers, the invisible children's bright high voices, that eternal playground sound, floating across the railway lines towards me on the now unsmoky, unpolluted, cleaned-up Oldbury air.

The Degrees of Life

What are the degrees of life in a plastic cowboy, say, or a snail? A dog is alive, a ladybird. Is a digger? My Dinky car goes, 'Brm brm!' My teddy talks. If something moves, is it alive? If it makes a noise? The kettle whistles on the hob. The lavatory makes a sucking, gurgling noise. It could suck you down, suck you in. If a thing can suck you in, is it alive?

I am a ventriloquist, lending my voice to a dozen little toys, helping them to live their lives. I play with them, they play with me. They wait for me in my room, in my bed. They behave badly. I forgive them. My teddy is as old as me. I am cruel to him sometimes. I am cruel to the cat. I make her wear a baby's hat or my teddy's scarf. I drop my teddy out of the window down into the yard. Is my teddy alive? I tell my friend when we are playing in the yard, 'You hear a horse!' I gallop up to him. He shoots me. I am dead. Then I am alive again. His mother smacks him round the head as he rides by. For something.

Tiny ants down in the dirt. I block their way with a matchstick or sweet wrapper. A blob of spit. Ants are alive. Grass grows. Rhubarb grows. Things smaller than ants inhabit the dirt, almost invisible. A mould spreads out on a bruised apple. Is a mould alive?

What is the degree of life in a beetle? A beetle goes crunch beneath the sole of my shoe. Another boy – not me! – pulls wings off butterflies, off moths. The legs off a spider. They crawl or limp away, still alive. I rescue a spider in the lavatory. He scuttles up a piece of paper. I shake him out into the garden.

At the Saturday Cinema Club I watch *Flash Gordon and the Claymen*. Are the Claymen alive? They appear out of the walls in the underground city, or blend back into them. Alive. Not alive.

Mrs Smith has a baby. My mother takes me against my will to see it. In Mrs Smith's big bed with Mrs Smith. Inside of Mrs Smith the week before. Was the baby alive?

Our house on Cemetery Road. The black hearse crawling by. The coffin. The body. Is the body alive? Does it die and come alive again? If you shoot it, can it jump back up?

Bedtime. A living wind outside the house. A shifting shadow in a corner of the room. The curtains move. I wrap one arm around my teddy for both our sakes and tell him my important things. This, that and the other. Is Teddy alive? Just a little, as much, say, as a Clayman or an ant, or a beetle, or an unborn baby?

Yes, says Teddy. He thinks he is.

The Richest Woman in the World

There was a door that you came in through, counters left and right, a spider's web of wires above your head and a glass box at the far end up a flight of stairs with a woman in it: the richest woman in the world.

It was the Co-op. There was sawdust on the floor. My mother bought bacon and cheese, eggs and butter, brown sauce, scoops of things out of barrels. Dog biscuits. (A lot of 'b's'!) Reluctantly, it seemed to me, she opened her purse and handed her money to the man. He wore an apron and had a pencil behind his ear. He put the money in a metal pot, screwed it up on to an overhead wire, pulled a chain – like a lavatory chain – and shot the money off. It whizzed up to the woman in the glass box. She opened it and kept the money, while returning any necessary change. Other men and women served other women and men. Other kids stood gazing up, desperate to get their hands on this spring-loaded, toy-like contraption. The air was full of flying money.

You could not really see the woman. Light reflecting from the glass box obscured her. I never saw her go into or come out of it. Yet I understood this well enough. It was no mystery to me. She was too busy counting her money.

My Invisible Dad

My dad is a mystery
He has a bristly chin
His hat hangs in a house
That he is never in.

He goes to work at half-past five
Comes home at eight
I hear him whistling in the yard
His dinner on a plate

Gets dried out in the oven
He washes at the sink
Blows water like a walrus
His hairy ears are pink.

My dad makes model soldiers
He has a fretwork saw
His flat cap on the cabinet
His work boots by the door.

I smell his overalls
He leans above my cot
His whiskery kiss upon my cheek
His smoky breath is hot.

The light shines on the landing
Some music down below
Descending steps upon the stairs
From the dad I hardly know.

Fear of Eggshells

I was afraid in those days of eggshells, horseflies, the man with the thick tongue that would not fit into his mouth, the Pooles, earwigs and my own mother. There was a boy at school who had no friends. I wrote about him later:

> A friendless silent boy,
> His face blotched red and flaking raw,
> His expression infinitely sad.
>
> Some kind of eczema
> It was, I now suppose,
> The rusty iron mask he wore.
>
> But in those days we confidently swore
> It was from playing near dustbins
> And handling broken eggshells.[*]

Yes, and you can add dustbins to the list. A horsefly, of course, since it could kill a horse, could surely kill me. Earwigs, by definition, crawled into your ear and burrowed their way into your brain, and ate it. Oh yes, and chewing

[*] 'The Boy Without a Name', *Heard it in the Playground*, extract (1989).

gum swallowed could strangle your heart. Add chewing gum.

The man with the thick tongue, in a flat cap and a mac (rain or shine), who wandered the streets like a Cyclops, one eye hooded over, the other glaring out; I was mortally afraid of him. The Pooles - I wrote about them too, called them the Toomeys - were a large family of sons, any one of whom could beat you to a pulp for no reason. They were a tribe, a pack, one a year in ascending order from babies up to grown men, from pram to pub. Even the toddler was tough, even the baby could make a fist.

I was afraid of the pigs in Marsh & Baxter's factory, squealing for their lives (afraid for them, you might say), the dark at the top of the stairs, that pool of thickening, malevolent air between the kitchen and my bed, and the hand which was under the bed waiting to grab my ankles. Yes, add the landing, add the pigs.

I was afraid of nursery rhymes:

> There was a little man
> And he had a little gun
> And his bullets were made
> Of lead, lead, lead.

He went to the brook
And saw a little duck
And shot it through
The head, head, head.

*

Bye, Baby Bunting
Daddy's gone a-hunting
To fetch a little rabbit skin
To wrap a Baby Bunting in.

*

Ladybird, Ladybird fly away home
Your house is on fire, your children are gone.

Yes, skinned rabbits, dead ducks, desolation.

Then there was my mother. My mother was a detective and a mind-reader. I'd cut the merest sliver of cake in the pantry, consume it to the last crumb, wash the knife, replace it in the drawer, and she'd know. She could look at me and turn my head to glass and see inside. Then I'd be for it. My mother hit me with whatever was handy, her hand mostly. A quick and stinging clip round the ear. There again, Trevor's mother hit him, I'm pretty sure. And Spencer's mother.

And when the mothers were weary of it, they'd tell the fathers when they came home from work, and the fathers would hit us. The teachers hit the big kids with a stick and little kids got smarting smacks to the tender calves of their little legs. The little kids, no doubt, copped it from the big kids too.

So, a clip round the ear from my old mum, who loved me and of whom I was afraid. She was very large when I was very small.

> When I was just a little child
> The world seemed wide to me
> My mum was like a feather bed
> My bath was like the sea.

My mother had a tiny birthmark high up on her forehead, almost in her hair. It resembled a bunch of grapes. She had her own distinctive smell: washing and ironing, the minty aroma of her medicine and Bible scent cards. She was also partially deaf in one ear from a blow to the head received in childhood. From *her* mother.

The Fishing

A garden cane, a cotton line
A matchstick and a pin
These were the things you needed
For the fishing to begin.

Secure the cotton to the cane
Bend the pin to a hook
Attach the matchstick for a float
Yes, this is what it took.

A chopped-up worm, or maggot
A ball of bread and spit
The park pond, grey and greenish
A place to squat or sit.

A waiting game, you watch your float
And eat a bit of bait
While light lies on the water
And fish swim up to their fate.

The little submarine fish
An inch or two, no more
Sticklebacks and minnows
Along that park pond shore.

Under that grey-green water's skin
Beneath your quivering float
With flickering fin and poppy-eyed
And bright red butcher's throat.

Hauled out at last into the air
(All for a mouthful of bread)
Deprived of life in the wide wild pond
Stuck in a jar instead.

A bloody hook, a ragged jaw
(All for a maggot-snack)
Though the stickleback has spines, y'know
With which to stab you back.

The park bell rings, the park gates close
You carry your catch away
And leave your jar in the wash house
And find it the following day.

A grey-green fish in the sunlight
Where its little corpse ascends
Floats belly up on the water's skin
And that is how it ends.

Seasons

There was a season for nesting
One wren's nest, full
Blown eggs and tiny labels
Shoebox and cotton wool.

A season for marbles
The losing, the winning
Glass balls of treasure
Light-filled, spinning.

There was a season for girlfriends
Kiss Chase and Truth or Dare
Maureen Copper's ankle socks
Plaid skirt and pig-tailed hair.

A season for butterflies
For conkers, for fire
Fire cans in November
Sparks thrown high and higher.

And a season for snow
Piled up at the door
Pressed faces at windows
Hoping for more.

We had snow then. Yes I know, I know, you're right, but we really did. In 1947 I opened the back door one morning and the snow was drifted up against the house and over my head. I made a modest living with our old pram fetching coke for Mrs Moore, and Margaret across the road. In the street we hurled our snowballs at the buses whenever they got through. And in the playground we turned the snow to ice . . . and slid on it.

THE MIGHTY SLIDE

The snow foams up around their feet,
And melts, too, in the friction's heat.
It changes once, it changes twice:
Snow to water; water to ice.

83

Now others arrive: the Fisher twins
And Alice Price. A queue begins.
The slide grows longer, front and back,
Like a giant high-speed snail's track,
And flatter and greyer and glassier, too,
And as it grows, so does the queue.
Each waits in line and slides and then
Runs round and waits and slides again.

And little is said and nothing is planned,
As more and more children take a hand
(Or a foot, if you like) in the slide's construction.
They work without wages and minus instruction.
Like a team of cleaners to and fro
With clever feet they polish the snow.
Like a temporary tribe in wintry weather,
They blow on their gloves and pull together.

[. . .]

And all the while from the frosty ground
That indescribable sliding sound.
Yes, snow's a pleasure and no mistake,
But the slide is the icing on the cake.*

* *The Mighty Slide*, extract (1988).

Cruelty to Animals

I knew a boy once who had a reputation. I put him and his reputation into a story. I called him Billy Harold. Billy, it was said, blew frogs up with a straw. I never saw him do it. Nobody saw him. He was, I suppose, for us a sort of Playboy of the Western World. It was his reputation.

All of us were cruel, of course, in varying degrees in those days. A generation of little boys laying waste to wildlife, and, in my case, the not-so-wild. The tiniest wren's eggs we took, piercing their delicate shells with equal delicacy, blowing their oft-times addled contents out on to the grass. Half-formed, aborted baby wrens. Or the pale fat maggots we pinned on our hooks, their creamy blood seeping forth (like wounded aliens, they were) on to our fingers. The upturned dying fish in our jam jars. The battered but still fluttering butterflies caught under our coats. The legless daddy-long-legs.

My personal cruelties were numerous, I fear, though I never touched a frog. Two episodes remain with me, however, to prick my conscience and serve me right. I was cruel to our cat, a good-natured, middle-aged tortoiseshell. I rolled her up in a towel sometimes, and turned her ears inside out (they soon flicked back). I buried her under the bedclothes and ignored her muffled miaows.

But worse than this or any of my 'naturalist's' crimes, worse than anything really, is what I did to the panda. When I was five or six, I took my well-loved soft toy panda into the wash house, soaked him under the tap, cleaned his ears out, scolded his grubby ways and mangled him. He went into the mangle round and came out flat. Not temporarily flat either, he was not well made to start with, but flat forever, hardly thicker than a slice of bread.

I work in a shed at the bottom of the garden. This shed contains many things: manuscripts, notebooks, dictionaries; a Prudential Assurance policy for the funeral expenses of a child (me); photographs, pencils, pens; a kettle; toy soldiers that my father did not make; an original 1940s clockwork boat with a key in its funnel that cost £375; a panda.

Yes, as I write these words, a crooked-eyed, glassy-eyed, eight-inch ancient panda is sitting on my desk. He is not my panda. My panda, remember, was mangled to a pulp. But he's of the tribe of panda. Actually, he's been on my desk for months, a candidate for a small part in another story. I'm auditioning him.

He gives me a look, had his eye on me, perhaps, for a while, before ever I thought to write this piece. A lopsided, reproachful look. Did you mangle the panda? (He sounds quite like my mother.) Did you flatten him out like a pancake, like pastry? Did you mangle him? Did you? I move him forward, lean him against a cup so that I can see him better. He looks pretty tough, it seems to me, for a soft toy. Time has dried him out, mangle-proofed him you might say, his head, especially, like a nut. And his gaze is full of accusations; implacable. Did you? Did you?

Well, yes, I did. I mangled the panda.

The Things I Ate

What did I eat when I was a boy
To make me the man I am?
Faggots 'n' peas and porridge, of course
Bread 'n' drippin' and jam.

And pencils, the paint to start with
Flakes of it, yellow and red
The wood, all soft and shredded
And, last but not least, the lead.

Dog biscuits, rubber bands, cardboard
A pear drop plus pocket fluff
I was a locust back then, it seems
And could not get enough.

Was it the sardines that built me up
And kept me so bony and thin?
The beans or Batchelors peas, perhaps
The molecules, even, of tin?

A lick of another kid's lolly
A sweet straight off the floor
A bite of another kid's apple
A beg of another kid's core.

Fish 'n' chips 'n' batters
Ketchup, vinegar, salt
Stick of rhubarb and sugar
Cod-liver oil and malt.

An ice cream at the pictures
Candyfloss at the fair
A bonfire-blackened potato
A brick-hard pilfered pear.

A baby cousin's abandoned rusk
A grandma's sip of stout
A sweet in its welded wrapper
An orange sucked inside out.

Was it the soap I swallowed
Or that half a ton of dirt
Curd tarts from Auntie Mabel
Humbugs from Uncle Bert?

Or even the air of Oldbury
That cloaked me from head to foot
A nose-tickling, eye-stinging, sulphurous soup
Peppered with sawdust and soot.

The fingernails I often chewed
The fingers I often ate
Bogies and blood from my own scraped knees
That lump of coal for a bet.

What did I eat when I was a boy
To make me the man I became?
If you'd fed me a different diet
Would I still have turned out the same?

All on account of a sausage
Or a secret swig of beer
Or a scab or suck of sherbet
Would I still be sitting here?

Poor Old Soul

Once more unto my mother, who, as it turned out, was not my mother. My mother was angry and strong. I would come home from school in the afternoon and find she'd moved a wardrobe. She had, as they say, an arm like a leg. Her anger, though, too often swung to violence. This was not all bad. One time Mrs Purnell caught us, me and Spencer, breaking bits of creosoted boards from her fence for Bonfire Night. It was pitch dark. She came out of her outside lavatory with a torch and fell on us like an avenging god.

'That's my fence, y' little buggers!'

She landed me a fearful swipe to the head.

'I'll teach you!'

I fell back on to Spencer. Mrs Purnell hauled me up.

'I'll give you bonfires!'

She was a mighty woman, half as big again as my mother, but, as we discovered, not so tough. Mum was there, in her apron and one slipper.

'Hey!' She grabbed my arm and pulled me free. Mrs Purnell advanced. Mum stood firm.

'Bloody kids!'

'My kids,' said Mum, briefly it seems adopting Spencer. 'Hit your own.'

Undeterred Mrs Purnell came on.

'Bloody bonfires!'

Spencer and I were tucked in behind my mother, like baby ducklings. Mrs Purnell sought to hit us with a broken board.

'Hey!' Mum grabbed the board and hit her with it.

Mrs Purnell staggered back, dropped her torch, and – 'Bloody cow!' – retreated.

That was me, aged eight. When Mum was eight, her mother took her to a doctor's surgery at half-past seven in the morning, before school, to scrub the floor or help her mother scrub it, I suppose. When she was fourteen, her mother altered her birth certificate, changing the date (in August) so that she could leave school and get a job. She had two birthdays after that, Mum said, like the Queen.

When I was ten, this happened. A gang of us were playing in the street. A girl, responding to some spiteful act of mine, perhaps, or out of meanness, taunted me. 'Your mother,' she'd overheard an auntie saying, 'your mother *is not your mother*.'

What an odd business. This news about my mother was news to me – a bombshell! – yet, there again, once told I never doubted it for an instant. That girl's bright voice –

Audrey her name was, or Gillian? – so vehement, so full of force, like a slap.

Home I ran with burning face and ears, down the dark entry into the house. Mum was in the kitchen listening to the wireless with the lights off, Dad round at the pub, Dinah asleep on the hearthrug. Mum rose from her chair, about to berate me for the lateness of the hour. I beat her to it. My mother, who was not my mother, I see her now, her raw red cleaner's hands twisting away at her apron as she struggled to speak. Adoption was a shameful business then in many people's eyes, the babies being mostly illegitimate. Better not speak of it. Eventually, her altogether collapsing face. Her tears. Her reaching out, my flinching away. And the love she urged me to believe in. And the years it took for me to do so.

My mother, who *was* my mother, loved me. I know this now. When I was forty-eight and she was eighty-two, and I was bigger and she was smaller (a leg like an arm), stoical, unselfpityingly, my mother died. In a hospital bed with a tube in her arm and a tube in her nose. Me beside her holding her hand. She is barely there, but produces for me a wry half-smile, acknowledging the tubes and her predicament. Meanwhile, along the ward between the rows of beds, another elderly patient advances with a Zimmer frame. Mum watches, nods in her direction and smiles again. 'Look at her,' she says, and squeezes my hand. 'Poor old soul.'

And here's another of *The Clothes Horse* stories that I wrote, or that popped up out of itself, so to speak. I'd always intended to fit it in somewhere. This seems as good a place as any.

LIFE SAVINGS

There was once a woman who decided to save parts of her life till later, when she might have more need of them. She had the idea when she was quite young, and her parents encouraged her. The first part of her life she ever saved was half an hour from when she was four. Later, she saved a day from when she was five, another day from when she was five and a half, six days from when she was six . . . and so on, all the way through her life until she was seventy.

Well, she put all these life savings in a safe in her parents' office. (They had a fortune-telling business, with a little magic on the side.) Each one had its own special box with a label giving the duration – that means how long it was – and her age.

Eventually, as I said, the woman got to be seventy and decided to spend some of her savings. First she opened the box with a day in it from when she was eight. Her heart began to pound the moment the box was opened. She lost all interest in the office and the fortune-telling business, and rushed out into the park. Here she played on the swings and rolled on the grass and fished in the pond and ate ice cream. By the end of the day she was worn out, but her cheeks were rosy and her eyes shone.

The next morning after breakfast the woman opened the box with a week in it from when she was ten. After that a great deal happened – and a great deal didn't happen. Dusting didn't happen, for instance, or washing up or making an appointment at the hairdresser's. Not many bills were paid or weeds dug up. At the end of the week the woman needed another week to sort herself out. All the same her step was light as she walked about the town, and her friends said she was a changed woman.

Well, so it continued for some years with the woman spending her savings bit by bit. Not all her experiences were happy, of course; life is not like that. The two days from when she was fourteen, for instance, were dreadful. She felt terribly shy all the time and was desperately worried about an almost invisible spot on her chin.

Then, finally, when she had used up all her life savings, the woman took to her bed, read a book for a while and – presently – died.

Some days later when friends were clearing out the office, one box of the woman's savings was discovered unopened. It was tucked away under a pile of old letters in the safe. The woman herself must not have noticed it. Its label (in her father's hand) said: Half an hour, age four.

Well, as soon as the box was opened, odd things began to happen. One of the friends went racing up and down the stairs – the office was on the third floor;

another made a den under the desk, and a third played with the phone.

Of course, as you will realize, it was the last half-hour of the woman's life that was causing this. Now that the woman herself was dead, it had nowhere else to go and, apparently, no reason to come to an end. In fact, as far as I know, it's still around . . . somewhere.

So, there we are. If ever you should feel the urge to act like a four-year-old (unless you are a four-year-old), you can blame it on the life savings of the woman in the fortune-telling business, with a little magic on the side. That's what I'd do.*

97

*The Clothes Horse and Other Stories (1987).

Street Lamps

The street lamps of my childhood
Are gas-lit, yellow and green
A series of safe havens
With darkness in between.

On winter nights when I come home
From the chip shop or the park
The shadows lengthen between the lamps
And I feel the clutch of the dark.

It's foggy, perhaps, rain in the air
An ebony pavement that gleams
Privet hedges, garden gates
But nothing is what it seems.

A limping man in the lamplight
With a scar or a blackened eye
A smoker or cougher or spitter of phlegm
An uninnocent passer-by.

A cat in a hedge, or something
A pair of eyes at least
A foot-dragging sound in an entry
Some nameless lurking beast.

While under each glowing umbrella
I shelter from the dark
With my hot chips from the chip shop
My cold feet from the park.

There's a ruffian in the entry
A hunchback at my heel
I run for my life in stages
For fear that my fears are real.

An iron tree, a cross bar
(Where the lighter's ladder leant)
A glass box with a pointed top
Like a small transparent tent.

The terrors of life await us
They lurk in the shadows between
The islands of hope and brightness
The pools of yellow and green.

"I DON'T want this silly old bear in *my* Family," cried Doreen, flinging Woodle Bear across the room.

"And I don't want this silly old bear in *my* Family either," returned Pris, flinging him back again.

Woodle Bear fell with a bump right into the middle of Doreen's Family of Toys, who were all sitting upright with their backs to the wall waiting to be taken out for a ride in the doll's pram.

Reading and Writing

I have a book. It is a book of Woodle Bear. And I am Woodle Bear. And Woodle Bear is me.

There weren't many books in our house, when I was a boy. I seem to have acquired them at the rate of one a year, as Sunday School prizes. Starting at the age of four or five, by the age of ten I had a library of six books. There was a book about Banjo the Crow; a book about a Berkshire pig abandoned by his owner and left to have adventures on the high veldt and in the steaming jungles of South Africa. There was a book about Woodle Bear.

The Bear Nobody Wanted
Written and Illustrated by
G. E. BREARY

Flap copy: Although Woodle was a handsome Bear in a new red coat, Doreen and Pris didn't want him and flung him out of the nursery window. Woodle was very sad; a Bear has to live somewhere, but where could he go? You will read here of his exciting adventures until at last he becomes King of Fairyland!

3 shillings net.

Well, this small book, 5" x 7", paper jacket, orange binding, 48pp, got its hooks into me from the very start.

> Woodle Bear fell with a bump right into the middle of Doreen's Family of Toys, who were all sitting upright with their backs to the wall waiting to be taken out for a ride in the doll's pram.
>
> They all looked at the little Bear in a superior sort of way, for they all knew that Doreen wanted *them* in her Family very much indeed.

Yes. I was Woodle Bear, all right, and Woodle Bear was me. The story had a potent effect on me. I loved to read and read again about those nasty girls. They had a 'nursery', they had a 'porch'. And the words said things like 'very much indeed' and '*returned* Pris'. (What could that mean?) But the fate of Woodle Bear, even though I knew the happy ending, was dreadful to contemplate. You will see where this piece is headed. I was an adopted child, but, age five, I didn't know it. Or did I?

A lifetime later, having parted company with and pretty well forgotten this book, though not its title, I chose, for reasons I can hardly fathom, to write my own version:[*] 6" x 9", paper jacket, orange binding, 144pp.

[*] *The Bear Nobody Wanted* (1992), £9.99.

THE BEAR
NOBODY WANTED

Janet and Allan Ahlberg

VIKING

This is how a bear was made many years ago. The materials used were: brown plush for the fur, velvet or felt for the paws, and strong black thread for the nose and mouth. In addition the following things were needed: one pair of glass eyes, five disc joints for attaching the head, arms and legs to the body, and lots of kapok or wood wool for the filling. Sometimes an extra item such as a squeaker was included. Ribbons, too, usually red and in the form of a bow, were popular then.

Woodle Bear was not wanted because Doreen and Pris were mean-spirited girls. My bear was not wanted for a more intractable reason; the circumstances, you might say, of his birth, or more particularly his conception.

Now the particular bear this story is about was made in a teddy bear factory. Here at a long table a number of women or young girls would sit. (You could start work at fourteen in those days.) Each would make one part of the bear, or concentrate on the sewing, filling or whatever, then pass it on to the next. In this way, the materials – plush and kapok, velvet and thread – moved down the table slowly taking on the shape and appearance of a bear. The bears, as it were, *materialized* from the piles of stuff and the busy fingers of the women.

Every stage in the process was important, but one stage was vital. This was the stitching of the nose and mouth, and the positioning of the eyes. The women who did this job were called 'finishers', and theirs was the most skilled work of all. Just one slip with the needle or mistake in the positioning of the eyes could change a bear's expression from cheerful to grumpy, trustworthy to sly, and ruin his life forever. For how a bear looked, especially when he was new, was how he *was*. His character was formed from the outside. It isn't fair, I know. It was hardly a bear's fault if things went wrong. But that is how it was.

Well, as you will see, the particular bear this story is about was to suffer in just this way. For as soon as his eyes were in his head, and his nose and mouth were stitched below them, this little bear was filled with a sense of his own importance (as filled he was with kapok). All of us have this feeling, of course, to some extent; but with this bear the conviction was too strong. It made him instantly proud and selfish. A couple of misplaced stitches, that's all it took; a bit of crookedness about the eyes, and the job was done.

But back to G. E. Breary's original, with which, you will have guessed, I am now reacquainted. It's in my hand again, the same 1940s edition. It has that ancient-paper smell. My first copy had a smell too, of damp. It was permanently damp in the upper rooms of our cold house: steam rising from kettles and cooking, tin baths in front of the fire, clothes drying on the clothes horse. The condensation then might have come back down as rain if only the ceilings had been higher. Paper of all kinds had a soggy time of it in those days.

And Woodle? He triumphs in the end, of course, returning to the porch resplendent in a jewelled crown, satin cloak, silver sword.

One day he flew down to the porch on which he had spent such a sad day long ago. Doreen and Pris were playing with their toys in the garden. Doreen saw him first.

'Look!' she cried excitedly, 'there is a lovely little Bear on the porch dressed in a satin cloak!'

'Goodness! I must get him, I do want him so,' cried Pris, running off to fetch a ladder.

'I do want him so.' I liked that, though the 'so' was something of a puzzle when I was six. There again, at this distance, there are other larger puzzles. Why did this book have such a hold on me? What were my feelings, reading it, that I cannot now quite recollect or draw back up? What were my *presentiments*?

As each bear completed his journey down the table, he was put on a trolley with the others. Here he had a grandstand view of more bears being made, and could begin to puzzle out his surroundings (and his own existence).

It was a curious business with new-made bears. Only a little while ago they had been piles of fabric, spools of thread, sacks of kapok. And yet now here they were, *knowing* things. I suppose it was a sort of instinct, really. The way a baby bird, for instance, will crouch when it sees the shadow of a hawk. Whatever it was, these new-made bears knew things from the start; not just that they were 'bears' or 'made', but other things, too. Words like 'shop' and 'pre-

sent' already had some meaning for them; words like 'child'
as well, and 'bedtime' and 'belonging'.

I'm in my shed now, writing this. It's August. A small view
of the garden, a blackbird on the grass and G. E. Breary's
paper-jacketed, musty-smelling, written *and* illustrated
good book in my other hand. The endpaper is cream. It
has the dealer's reference number pencilled lightly in the
top right corner. And the word 'child'. And the amount,
£40. Forty pounds, that's less than a pound a page, isn't it?
Yes. Worth every penny.

An Elemental Childhood

I lower my bucket down into the well and draw up . . . water. Water was thicker in my childhood, time has diluted it. It came in coils and cables out of the mouths of drinking fountains and flooded, leaf-clogged gutterings. Small boys could pee with it halfway up a wall. It was like barley sugar or rope. Sometimes when it rained, it fell in soft fat lumps, impacting on the park pond (while we took shelter in the sheds), pockmarking its surface but not breaking it. The skin on the water, like the skin on a grape; a matchstick float could lie on top of it and would require some powerful fishy force to drag it under. Insects, water boatmen and such, bounced on or tiptoed over it as though it were a trampoline; flat pebbles skimmed it. Sometimes the raindrops were so fine, gravity could not draw them down. They hung suspended around the yellowish, greenish street lamps in glowing spheres, like jellyfish.

Water fought a battle with the earth – or dirt, as I more familiarly regarded it – for the possession of my small body. My fingernails were full of it. It was tattooed into my elbows and scabby knees, silted up between my toes. Mum scrubbed away at me, sluiced me down, corkscrewed my ears with a twist of towel, licked her hankie and wiped my face like cleaning a window. The dirt returned. Dirt was my friend. I played with it, rolled in it sometimes, like a dog. I ate it even, once in a while, when a biscuit or boiled sweet ended up on the ground and no adult was there to talk me out of picking it up.

And now there's air in my bucket. It too has weight. Coming down off the Rounds Green Hills or from Dudley Castle, you'd hold your nose and dive back in. An atmosphere, a soup, cooked up to the town's own recipe. Oldbury was a place you could walk around with your eyes shut and know where you were. British Industrial Plastics, Guest, Keen and Nettlefolds, The Brades, each had its own aroma. There was a glue factory that boiled up bones. The canals – Oldbury was a sort of Venice – were green and scummy. Marlholes bubbled away like New Zealand geysers and glowed in the dark. The smells were sulphurous, hot-metalled, lead-filled, but also, surely, medicinal. Microbes and germs had as tough a time as we did in those days, in that inoculated air.

Finally, there was fire. Fire was a fascination when I was seven or eight. I was a moth to it. Matches were treasure. We traded for them, begged them, stole them. Any form of fire would do, any sort of fuel. We cooked and ate potatoes; burnt black, half-raw, delicious. There was the smell of singed teddies, the whooshing disappearance altogether of a celluloid frog, burning rubber. Best of all, most memorably of all, there was fire in a can.

A fire can was a serious delight to me: portable fire! To make one you needed a can, a hammer, a six-inch nail and wire for the handle. Hammer some holes into the can, fill it up with paper, twigs, rabbit-hutch straw, firewood splinters, bits of coal. Set it alight and . . . swing. The rush of air was like a bellows. Sometimes a well-made can glowed red hot and melted. Sparks flew and boys set light to themselves; eyebrows and even eyes were lost.

And so it was. Our fires sent ashes and soot high up into the air, rain washed it all back down, brown rivulets on windowpanes and pavements, the earth soaked it up. The sun shone forth (as best it could) and dried things out, steam and dust motes rising. A circular engine, a swirl of ancient molecules round and round, the whole town in a permanent smoky flux, like a Turner painting. And me – who else? – slap bang, stage front in the middle of it.

Ends

What puts an end to childhood, of course, is time and, in my case also, football. The ref blew his whistle, you might say, and something else kicked off.

The power of any particular memory is, I have found (or seem to remember), in inverse proportion to the amount of detail it contains. There's a lot of detail in this book, it's crammed with it, but the memories that matter most are the ones I've had to stretch for, that shimmer on the edge of things: pillowcase, green light under the table, Dad's dancing overalls. And once you arrive at a certain age, the memories of that age come thick and fast and fully clothed. You have no need of a bucket to draw them up, it's all on tap.

Football: it was the extended orderliness of it, I think, that did away with my childhood. Its all-encompassingness. The gathering together of a team to play another team, the distribution of positions – how many centre forwards could one team possibly have? – the boots, the ball, the dubbin. And the leaving of the house, the demarcation of the pitch – coats for goals, trees, paths and shrubberies for touchlines – getting lost in a tribal ebb and flow in an ever-darkening park for hours and hours, till the bell rang and the keeper on his bike obliged us to leave.

So leave we did, and more than the park and the pitch were left behind, I'd say. Of course, you're right – you mostly are – we were still children and it was still childhood. But there again somehow mysteriously . . . not. The crossing of that line between the little kids and the kids, it happens to us all, and always when we are not looking. A chalk line in the playground rubbed out by running feet. A curtain coming down behind us. When I was five, could I remember being four or three? When three, remember two or one? When one . . .? The fugitive pictures fade. Goodbye, Teddy, toy soldiers, clothes-horse-in-the-kitchen den. Goodbye, goodbye. I'm off to kick a ball.

In the poem which follows* I should point out (for the purposes of the present book) that Albert Park was not Albert Park. There was (is) no Albert Park. It was West Smethwick Park. There was no boy named Tommy Gray either, or Briggs. Rhythm and rhyme had a hand in team selection. For that matter, alliteration – Rover, Rex and Roy – was influential, not to say decisive, in the naming of the dogs.

* In *Friendly Matches* (2001).

THE MATCH (c. 1950)

The match was played in Albert Park
From half-past four till after dark
By two opposing tribes of boys
Who specialized in mud and noise;

Scratches got from climbing trees
Runny noses, scabby knees
Hair shaved halfway up the head
And names like Horace, Archie, Ted.

The match was played come rain or shine
By boys who you could not confine
Whose common goals all unconcealed
Were played out on the football field.

Off from school in all directions
Sparks of boys with bright complexions
Rushing home with one idea
To grab their boots . . . and disappear.

But Mother in the doorway leaning
Brings to this scene a different meaning
The jobs and duties of a son
Yes, there are *errands to be run.*

Take this wool to Mrs Draper
Stop at Pollock's for a paper
Mind this baby, beat this rug
Give your poor old mum a hug.

Eat this apple, eat this cake
Eat these dumplings, carrots, steak!
Bread 'n' drippin', bread 'n' jam
Mind the traffic, so long, scram.

Picture this, you're gazing down
Upon that smoky factory town.
Weaves of streets spread out, converge
And from the houses boys emerge.

Specks of boys, a broad selection
Heading off in one direction
Pulled by some magnetic itch
Up to the park, on to the pitch.

Boys in boots and boys in wellies
Skinny boys and boys with bellies
Tiny boys with untied laces
Brainy boys with violin cases.

The match was played to certain rules
By boys from certain streets and schools
Who since their babyhood had known
Which patch of earth to call their own.

The pitch, meanwhile, you'd have to say
Was nothing, just a place to play.
No nets, no posts, no *lines*, alas
The only thing it had was grass.

Each team would somehow pick itself
No boys were left upon the shelf
No substitutions, sulks or shame
If you showed up, you got a game.

Not 2·3·5 or 4·2·4
But 2·8·12 or even more.
Six centre forwards, five right wings
Was just the normal run of things.

116

Lined up then in such formations
Careless of life's complications
Deaf to birdsong, blind to flowers
Prepared to chase a ball for hours,

A swarm of boys who heart and soul
Must make a bee-line for the goal.
A kind of ordered anarchy
(There was, of course, *no* referee).

They ran and shouted, ran and shot
(At passing they were not so hot)
Pulled a sock up, rolled a sleeve
And scored more goals than you'd believe.

Slid and tackled, leapt and fell
Dodged and dribbled, dived as well
Headed, shouldered, elbowed, kneed
And, half-time in the bushes, peed.

With muddy shorts and muddy faces
Bloody knees and busted laces
Ruddy cheeks and plastered hair
And voices buffeting the air.

Voices flung above the trees
Heard half a mile away with ease,
For every throw in, every kick
Required an inquest double quick.

A shouting match, all fuss and fury
(Prosecutors, judges, jury)
A match of mouths set to repeat
The main and muddier match of feet.

Thus hot and bothered, loud and nifty
That's how we played in 1950
A maze of moves, a fugue of noise
From forty little boiling boys.

Yet there was talent, don't forget
Grace and courage too, you bet
Boys like Briggs or Tommy Gray
Who were, quite simply, born to play.

You could have stuck them on the moon
They would have started scoring soon
No swanky kit, uncoached, unheeded
A pumped-up ball was all they needed.

Around the fringes of the match
Spectators to this hectic patch
Younger sisters, older brothers
Tied-up dogs and irate mothers.

A mother come to claim her twins
(Required to *play* those violins).
A little sister, Annabelle
Bribed with a lolly not to tell.

Dogs named Rover, Rex or Roy
Each watching one particular boy.
A pup mad keen to chase the ball
The older dogs had seen it all.

The match was played till after dark
(Till gates were closed on Albert Park)
By shadowy boys whose shapes dissolved
Into the earth as it revolved.

Ghostly boys who flitted by
Like bats across the evening sky,
A final fling, a final call
Pursuing the invisible ball.

The match was played, the match *is* over
For Horace, Annabelle and Rover.
A multitude of feet retrace
The steps that brought them to this place.

For gangs of neighbours, brothers, friends
A slow walk home is how it ends,
Into a kitchen's steamy muddle
To get a shouting at . . . or cuddle.

See it now, you're looking down
Upon that lamp-lit factory town.
It's late (it's *night*) for Rex or Ted
And everybody's gone to bed.

Under the rooftops slicked with rain
The match is being played again
By two opposing well-scrubbed teams
Who race and holler in their dreams.

I'm in my shed; early morning, late September. Once in a while an apple thuds down on to the roof. Pigeons land and walk about; I hear their scratchy feet. The book is finished, if not quite finished off. It shouldn't take long, though it could in theory take forever. There's probably a Borges story on the subject. The man who wrote a book, and who went through it at the end giving it a scrub, tidying it up, adding and subtracting. And then continued, correcting the corrections, the corrections, the corrections. This is how a book was made many years ago. The materials used were ... and the materials *not* used?

> There's a man on West Bromwich market
> At certain times of the year
> With a hat made out of feathers
> And a stall that you can *hear.*

Day-old Chicks: for instance, I more or less promised right at the beginning 'day-old chicks'. So where are they? The rag-and-bone man used to give them away in exchange for a sufficient quantity of stuff. (Also – just remembered – paper windmills!) And we kept hens. I collected the eggs, helped my mother to boil the potato peelings, mix the mash. My mother, on one occasion to my absolute horror, put a dying day-old chick *in the oven*. But, as I quickly realized, only to revive it. My way in, however, my preferred approach to the chicks, was that stall on West Bromwich market, that noisy stall:

I hear it in the street outside
And slip my mother's hand
And dodge along the gangways
To muscle in and stand

On tip toe; I can just see in
The stall's like a giant tray
With sawdust, little drinking troughs
And a lamp as bright as day.

Yes. Then I got stuck. It took me a time to realize it wasn't, in this instance, the chicks I was really interested in, or the stall, it was The Market. The cathedral-like, Bingley Hall-like space; an enormous, roofed-in world to run around in, free of my mother's hand. It's more than likely, by the way, that I made up the hat.

Snail Hunt: This is the fourth shed I have owned in my working life. Like all the others, it is lined out with pinboard, allowing me to pin things up (photographs, letters, work), encircle myself in a paper castle. There's a newspaper cutting: How I Found Bliss in My Shed at 6.05am; a photograph of my dad, uncharacteristically in a suit and tie at a wedding. And a letter from Jessica, where, aged five or so, she proceeds to reinvent herself, enlarging her family and putting me to work in a shop.

No, on closer reading, it's worse than that. I'm merely the addressee. Her father *is* the shopman. I've been written out.

At what age, how early, do we begin to reinvent ourselves, rearrange the story, take it over? I met a small child recently, named Norah. She was fifteen months old. Her first word to me, indeed almost her only word, was 'up'. She liked our house, which is tall and thin. 'Up!' she would say, and point. And up we'd go. She, with increasing skill, stair by stair. Me, hovering. In one of the bedrooms there was a free-standing mirror. Norah and I played with the mirror. We kissed ourselves in it and laughed at the absurdity of kissing ourselves. Norah held her soft toy, a giraffe, up to the mirror, and the giraffe kissed itself. Norah laughed again. It was a play, a play to be repeated (and revised) as often as she wished, of kissing toys and things alive in mirrors.

Jessica's letter, now twenty-seven years old, is faded, yellowed, but also, more recently along its bottom edge, nibbled at. It took me a time to notice what was happening and work out the cause. It was snails, tiny snails that got in under the door, scaled the walls and ate my papers.

Dear Allan Ahlberg
Yes I can swim
I do Go to
School my nase teacher
is a man. my mum Gos
to The hospital
and my dad is a Shop man
I have got
Tim and Joan and Jane and
Tommy I live in a
flat We have bunk
debs.

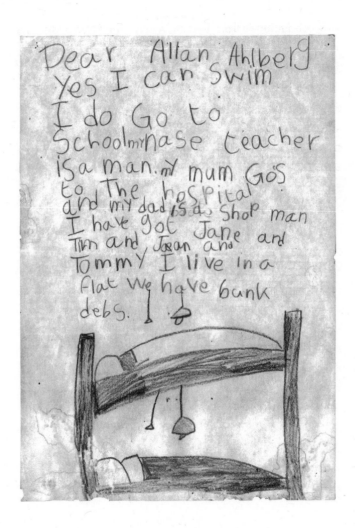

Snails are slow eaters who hide out in the daytime, though left alone for long enough this particular tribe would surely have grazed their way across the walls, the shelves, the desk. This book itself, this earliest handwritten draft (do they like ink?) presently beneath my hand, would eventually in time have been chomped up and turned into snail. Snails are cunning creatures. There again, deceiving a grown man is one thing, but 'when you are little you *see* the little'. They'd never have got away with it when I was four.

The Warmth of the Bed: I will end (I seem to have been promising this for a while) with a couple of late additions and a dedication. I have a picture in my head: me with my mum and dad at the table, Dad peeling an apple. He uses his pocket knife and completes the process in one continuous spiralling curl of green. (It's always a green apple.) That's the challenge, of course, to remove the peel, all of it, unbroken. Then we eat the apple. Then we eat the peel. Two different tastes and textures for the price of one, distinguished and revealed by my clever dad. He takes an apple in his 'cracked and cut and calloused' hand and turns it into a conjuring trick.

And the second scene: The Warmth of the Bed. With this one, it's pretty well all there in the title. Jumping into my parents' bed just after the last of them – my mother, usually – has left it. The hugeness of the bed, weight of blanket and quilt, surrounding sea of chilly lino. The after-glow of somebody else's body, the after-shape of it ... dinted. (In his master's steps he trod, where the snow lay dinted.) A warm impression, encoded on my skin, perhaps; a brief remembrance of living heat. Like climbing into a hot pie.

Dedication: I propose to make a bit of a display here and, to this end, have commissioned artwork from Jessica. Here it is:

Two mothers, two fathers and me like a parcel or a baton (or a hot potato!) passed between them. There are mysteries at the bottom of the world for all of us. In such a context, four parents is hardly more remarkable than two. In any case, at this great distance I love them all. My stoical mother, who ran the home, paid the insurance, cleaned the houses, scrubbed the floors. My half-visible, selfless dad, a working man, who all his life got up and went to work. My other mother, unmarried, too young to be a mother, really; my other father . . . unknown.

And yet I fancy I look a bit like him. I bet I do – or her. And which one of them was it put a pen in my hand (a pencil behind my ear), or passed on – one touch – my phenomenal football skills? Where did my whistling come from? It took four finishers to finish me off, stitch in my nose and mouth, position my eyes, tie my ribbon. I have no wish – though this must sound complaisant – ever to complain at all, about the outcome.

It's the end of *The Bear Nobody Wanted*: the bear has found his final home. A boy named Trevor has rescued him from the horrors of a bombed-out building, cleaned him up and made a present of him to his little sister.

> Sophie snuggled down with the bear in her arms and the rabbit on her pillow. She began to talk: 'It's Sunday School tomorrow . . . My daddy is a sailor.'

After a while, Trevor put his head round the door. He came over to the bed and crouched beside it. Sophie held the bear up for them to see each other. Trevor shook him by the paw.

'What will you call him?' he whispered.

'I will call him . . . Teddy,' Sophie said.

Trevor left, and slowly Sophie drifted off to sleep. Her arm remained around the bear and her warm breath touched his fur. With only the slightest movement of his paw, the bear returned her cuddle. He would not sleep for ages yet. His heart and mind were just too full. He was, of course, the happiest of toys: an altogether *wanted* bear.

It is particularly requested that this Policy be carefully read and at once returned to the Company should any correction be necessary. It is important that any change of name or address should be notified in writing to the Agent.

THE

PRUDENTIAL

ASSURANCE COMPANY LIMITED.

(Incorporated in England).

CHIEF OFFICE—HOLBORN BARS, LONDON, E.C.1.

INDUSTRIAL BRANCH.

Form 2578.

1 C

Whole Life Assurance on Life of Another for Funeral Expenses with Bonus Participation as stated below.

Free for reduced amount after one year's premiums have been paid.

Ages 1–10 next Birthday at entry.

Whereas a proposal has been made by the person named in the schedule hereto (hereinafter called " the Assured ") to effect an assurance upon the life of the child named in the said schedule who is stated in the proposal to be of the age specified in the said schedule (hereinafter called " the child ") with THE PRUDENTIAL ASSURANCE COMPANY LIMITED (hereinafter called " the Company ") on the terms hereinafter mentioned and on the basis of the aforesaid proposal. **And whereas** the assurance is effected for providing money to be paid for the funeral expenses of the child who is of the degree of relationship to the Assured stated in the said schedule. **Now these presents witness** that a premium of the amount specified in the said schedule having been paid to the Company on the granting of this Policy the Company hereby agree that if the Assured shall pay a premium of a similar amount to the Company or their duly authorised agent on or before or within twenty-eight days after the Monday succeeding the date of this Policy and every succeeding Monday during the life of the child or until the fulfilment of the provision in regard to age hereinafter contained then the Company will upon proof of death of the child and of the circumstances connected therewith being given to the reasonable satisfaction of the Directors of the Company pay the Benefit specified in the schedule to the Assured or the executors or administrators of the Assured.

After one year's premiums have been paid if a forfeiture notice under Section 23 of the Industrial Assurance Act 1923 is served and default made in payment of any premium to which the forfeiture notice relates in accordance with and within the period specified in such notice this Policy will on the expiration of the last-mentioned period automatically become a free paid-up Policy in respect whereof no premiums further be payable but under the conditions indorsed hereon will be payable and that the paid-up Policy will subject as hereinafter provided secure a reduced sum of an amount determined according to the Company's Tables for the time being in force for computing the amounts of free paid-up Policies to the Industrial Branch. Such reduced sum will not be less than the amount determined in accordance with the rules for ascertaining the amount of a free paid-up Policy contained in the 5th Schedule to the Industrial Assurance Act 1923. If after one year's premiums have been paid payment of premiums is discontinued with the intention of making no further payment then notwithstanding that no forfeiture notice is served this Policy will automatically become a free paid-up Policy securing such reduced sum as aforesaid provided that until service of a forfeiture notice and default made in payment of any premium thereunder this Policy may subject to the provisions and conditions of the same be restored to full benefit by payment of the premiums due thereon. The free paid-up Policy will secure the reduced sum only and will not participate in any bonus distribution made after such conversion. If after conversion into a free paid-up Policy the child shall under any age ten an assurance will be payable under the free paid-up Policy. When the Policy has become a free paid-up Policy the Company in certain cases as will in practice make to such assurance an indorsement on the Policy of a memorandum that it has become a free paid-up Policy for the reduced sum and stating the amount of that sum.

After premiums shall have been paid until the attainment by the child of age 75 the Policy in force will become a free paid-up Policy for the full sum assured and bonuses declared to the date when premiums cease to be payable.

The production by the Company of a receipt for any Benefit payable after the child has attained the age of ten years under this Policy or the conditions or statutory provisions indorsed hereon or under any free paid-up Policy which this Policy may have become which shall not have been paid during the lifetime of the Assured signed by any person being either an executor or administrator of the Assured or the husband or wife or a relative by blood or connection by marriage of the Assured shall be a good discharge to the Company for the same or against every person or persons whomsoever and every such receipt so signed as aforesaid shall be final and conclusive evidence to all intents and purposes that the Benefit therein expressed to have been received has been duly paid to and received by the person or persons lawfully and rightfully entitled to the same and that all claims and demands whatsoever against the Company in respect of such Benefit have been fully and truly satisfied and discharged.

The Company shall not be bound by any assignment (whether partial or otherwise) or mortgage of or charge on the Policy and shall be entitled to disregard the same and to deal only with or recognise only the Assured or such other person as are expressly authorised to give a receipt under the provision in that behalf hereinbefore mentioned.

This Policy is subject to the conditions and statutory provisions indorsed hereon and to the Articles of Association from time to time of the Company and will as annuals after it shall have become a free paid-up Policy as aforesaid. It is issued out of the Industrial Branch of the Company and the Industrial Branch Fund together with the Capital Stock of the Company shall alone be answerable for any claims hereunder.

This Policy is granted upon the express condition that the same absolutely void and all premiums paid thereon shall be forfeited to and retained by the Company if default shall be made in payment of the aforesaid premiums in compliance with the Statutory Notice of non-payment of a premium unless the Policy has become a free paid-up Policy as aforesaid or if any of the conditions indorsed hereon have not been or shall not be in all respects performed and observed.

WORLD WIDE.

See Free Policy Indorsement.

TABLE C.

SCHEDULE.

Nº OF POLICY.	NAME AND ADDRESS OF THE ASSURED.		
140165034 H50-1207	ELIZABETH AHLBERG 86 BIRCHFIELD LANE OLDBURY		
	NAME OF THE CHILD	Age next Birthday at Child stated at	RELATIONSHIP TO THE ASSURED
	GEORGE ALLAN AHLBERG	ONE year	CHILD
	SUM ASSURED PAYABLE AS DEATH SUBJECT TO THE CONDITIONS INDORSED HEREON		
AMOUNT OF WEEKLY PREMIUM. ONE PENNY			

As witness the common seal

of the Company this Twentieth

day of March one thousand

nine hundred and thirty nine

J. Bum
General Manager.

G. Hasbury

P. L. Reid.
Directors.